WERE YOU THERE

LONDON: HUMPHREY MILFORD

OXFORD UNIVERSITY PRESS

Were You There
When They Crucified My Lord

A Negro Spiritual in Illustrations by
Allan Rohan Crite

Cambridge, Massachusetts
Harvard University Press
· 1944 ·

STUDIO ADDICTUS
Province of Holy Cross

Dedicated to the memory of
the Reverend Father Frederick Cecil Powell, S.S.J.E.
Friend and Counselor

CONTENTS

INTRODUCTION

THE religious historian cannot fail to be impressed by the tide of devotion which he finds wherever his studies lead him. Throughout recorded history, mankind has used all the variety of his talents to the greater glory of his God: at the high moments in all forms of art we call that great which expresses the revelation through man of a more than human vision. Indeed, the history of religion is essential to the history of art, for who could appreciate the full beauty of the Acropolis, Michelangelo, or Bach without understanding the religious feeling of their times?

Music, of all the arts the most immediate in its appeal, has brought us some of the deepest expressions of religious feeling, and of these are the Spirituals of the American Negroes. Drawing on their own cultural heritage and on Methodist and Baptist protestantism, the Negroes have created out of their sufferings, their hopes, and their innate musical genius a body of original religious folk music which is universally loved for its vividness and power. Deeply serious works of spontaneous interpretation, sung unaccompanied by groups in the homes and in the fields as well as in the churches, the Spirituals are a moving expression of Christianity.

So universal is their appeal that many and varied attempts have been made to interpret them. Not all of these attempts have been fortunate, for popular taste has too often made over the Spirituals by adding harmonizations or accompaniments which destroy their peculiar freshness. But musical explorers have labored in late years to record this folk art in its original form, and audiences all over the world have been profoundly moved by the memorable interpretations of great singers of magnificent presence and dignity.

The book before us presents something of this cultural tradition in a different way. Here one of the best loved of all the Spirituals takes on the forms of life in the work of an artist whose birthright is an authentic understanding of the Spirituals, and who gives us that understanding in the terms of a dramatic and sensitive religious art. These pictures are not "illustrations" in the usual sense of visual elaborations of a text. They are rather a translation from one medium of expression to another, from musical rhythm into visual rhythm. Where the sung Spiritual creates cumulative dramatic tension by repeated variations of a musical phrase, the artist lays increasing stress on the central idea of a pictorial sequence. And just as no single phrase in music has real meaning apart from its context, so here the great story carries its full weight only in the interdependence of one picture upon the preceding and succeeding ones.

Indeed, as with unified compositions in all forms of art, no one perusal will reveal the whole significance of this book. The reader may first scan the entire sequence rather rapidly, to feel the grand sweep of the story growing and coming to its climax. Then he may dwell on one of the episodes, moved, for example, by the ever-darkening finality of the Entombment. Or a particular picture may hold his attention by its portrayal, in the faces and poses of the figures, or in its artistic composition and religious symbolism, of an individual moment of feeling. Each new approach will deepen his appreciation.

As the thoughtful reader discovers the essential meaning of these pages, he will find that this great song lives again in its visual transposition. Here is sensitive understanding recorded by a sure hand, sincere experience devoutly interpreted, and deep feeling expressed with power and integrity. The Spiritual asks "Were you there?" These pictures are a moving answer to that question.

KENNETH JOHN CONANT

Cambridge
July 5, 1944

APOLOGIA

I HAVE long anticipated illustrating the Spirituals in such a way as to help create an atmosphere of peace and sacredness and time for reflection like that created by the words and music of the hymn. It has been my endeavor to bring out in these brush drawings that strong sense of vitality and reality that one senses in the Spirituals themselves.

To do this I have made use of the human figures as symbols. These figures set forth the various shadings and accents of the drama as it is suggested by the words and music. Usually a single figure represents the melody and groups of figures the accompaniment. The main motif is that of the suffering Christ, the secondary motifs or accompaniments are the Blessed Virgin Mary, St. John the Beloved Disciple, and the chorus in the background.

The wording "Were you there when they crucified my Lord?" implies the eternal aspect of the sacrifice of Christ, the character of which enables us who are born out of the historical time of the Crucifixion to be one with the peoples along the Via Dolorosa and to stand beneath the Cross. With this aspect in view, I made the figures of Our Lord, Mary, St. John, and the Roman soldiery in the traditional manner, but placed them in a modern setting. The figures of Simon the Cyrenean and St. Veronica, however, were done in ordinary modern dress, because these two characters stepped out of the crowd to render assistance to the Christ, and there have been men and women like Simon and St. Veronica in all ages, even down to today. In like manner the Women of Jerusalem are echoed repeatedly down through the pages of history. The illustrations portray the two natures of Christ, the human and the divine. Thus I have tried to show the two aspects of the Crucifixion, the historical incident and the Eternal Spiritual Act, both parts of which were suggested by the Spiritual.

The decorations facing the pictures are mostly in the usual tradition, although here and there I have taken some liberties. The entire procedure is governed by liturgy and religious iconography.

The entire Spiritual although narrative in character is at the same time contemplative. It continually asks the question "Were you there?"

ALLAN ROHAN CRITE

WERE YOU THERE

Were you there when they crucified...

My Lord......................................

Were you there when they crucified my Lord

O, sometimes it causes me to tremble O, tremble

Were you there when they crucified my Lord

Were you there when they nailed Him to the tree

Were you there when they nailed Him to the tree

O, sometimes it causes me to tremble

Tremble O Lord tremble.............

Were you there when they nailed Him to the tree

Were you there when they pierced Him in the side

Were you there when they pierced Him in the side

Sometimes it causes me to tremble

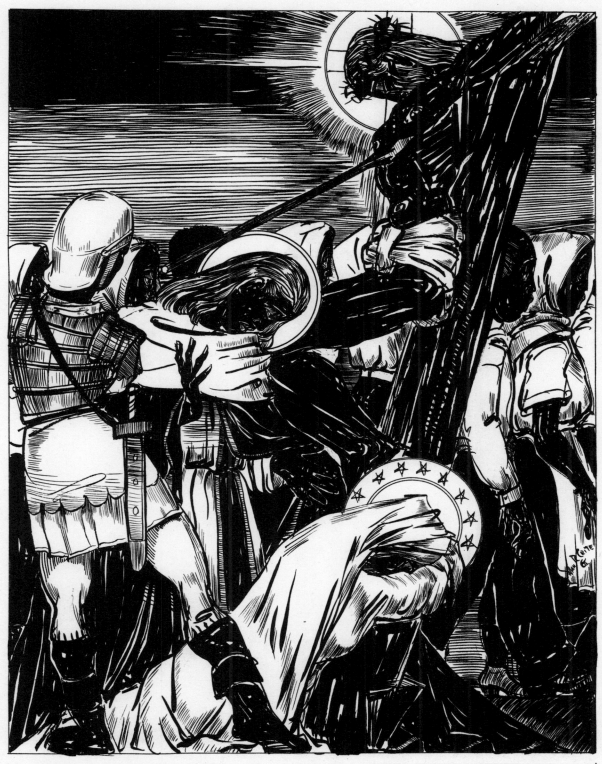

Tremble O Lord tremble...............

Were you there when they pierced Him in the side

Were you there when the sun refused to shine

Were you there when the sun refused to shine

Sometimes it causes me to tremble

Tremble O Lord tremble...............

Were you there when the sun refused to shine

Were you there when they laid Him in the tomb

Were you there when they laid Him in the tomb

O, sometimes it causes me to tremble

Tremble O Lord tremble..............

Were you there when they laid Him in the tomb

Were you there ....

When He rose from the dead...........

Were you there when He rose ....

................from the dead

O, sometimes it causes me to tremble, tremble

O tremble.......................

Were you there when He rose from the dead..

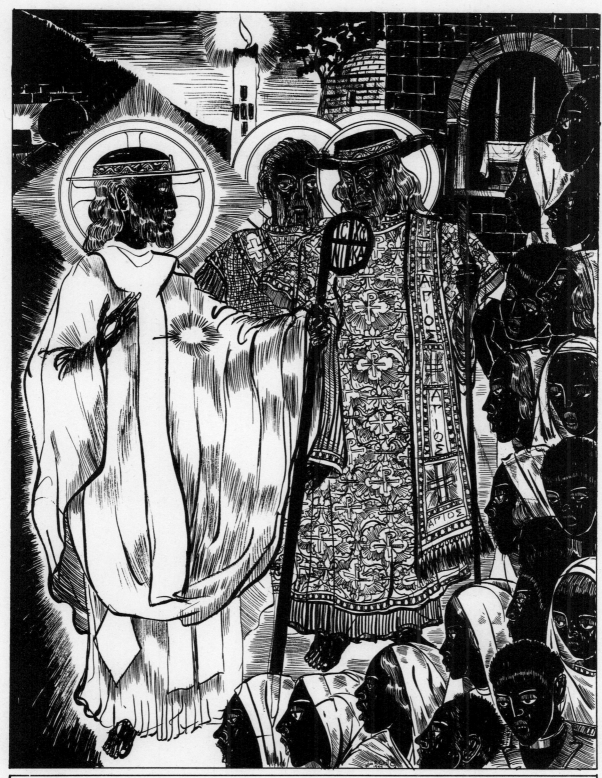

Were you there when He ascended on high

Were you there ....

When He ascended on high.........

O, sometimes it causes me to tremble

Tremble tremble ....

Were you there ....

When He ascended on high.........

7985

8342

7985